Technology All Around Us

Telecommunications

Anne Rooney

W
FRANKLIN WATTS
LONDON • SYDNEY

First published in 2005 by
Franklin Watts
96 Leonard Street
London EC2A 4XD

Franklin Watts Australia
Level 17/207 Kent Street
Sydney
NSW 2000

Produced by Arcturus Publishing Ltd,
26/27 Bickels Yard, 151-153 Bermondsey Street,
London SE1 3HA

Series concept: Alex Woolf
Editor: Alex Woolf
Designer: Simon Borrough
Picture researcher: Glass Onion Pictures

Picture Credits:
Corbis: 24 (Sergei Karpukhin), 25 (Aladin Abdel Naby), 26
(Panasonic Center/Handout).
Science Photo Library: 4 (Martin Riedl), 5 (Sheila Terry), 6
(Lawrence Lawry), 7 (Maximilian Stock Ltd), 8 (Hattie Young),
11, 14 (Mauro Fermariello), 16 (ESA/CE/Eurocontrol), 17 (Ken
M Johns), 18 (David Parker), 22 (Tek Image), cover and 28 (Dr
Seth Shostak), 29 (NASA).
Topham Picturepoint: 9 (PA), 10 (Ian Munro), 12, 13, 15
(UPPA), 19 (ImageWorks), 20 (ImageWorks), 21 (Ian Munro),
23, 27 (John Powell).

A CIP catalogue record for this book is available from the British
Library

ISBN 07496 5961 0

Printed in Singapore

Contents

We've all got used to being able to get in touch with our friends at the press of a few buttons. We rarely give a thought to the technology that makes this possible, called "telecommunications" systems.

Telecommunications – or telecoms – are a modern development and are still growing and changing rapidly. In a few years you'll be able to communicate in ways you probably don't dream of now.

Person to Person

We keep in touch by phone, email and text message, and use the radio, television and the World Wide Web to find out what's happening in the world. These technologies let us use the written or spoken word – and sometimes pictures or video – to communicate with each other.

Unlike letters, they are almost immediate. We can use them to hold a conversation over a long distance, as each message gets to its destination very quickly.

Using a mobile phone, we can chat to friends wherever we are.

>> Looking Forward

Email for the Himalayas

The simputer is a small, hand-held device that can be used for sending email or voice messages, or for web browsing. It can be used in any language, as the user writes on the screen with a plastic stylus.

The simputer was launched in 2004. Its developers hope that it will bring telecommunications to people in remote areas of the world, such as the Himalayas.

Machines Talking

Lots of electronic devices "talk" to each other, too. You could have a security system in your home that sends a message to your phone if an intruder breaks in, or you could buy a drink from a vending machine using your mobile phone.

Telecommunications are all around us – and becoming more and more important in our lives.

A Morse transmitter, used to send telegraphs. The operator uses the large button in the centre to tap out the code – a series of short and long signals – which are then sent by wire to a receiving machine. The receiving telex machine prints out the code as dots and dashes.

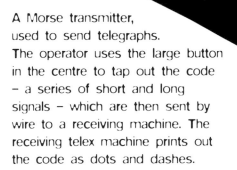

Looking Back

Telegraph

In 1830, American Joseph Henry sent an electric current along a mile of wire to ring a bell at the other end. This was the first telegraph and the start of modern telecommunications.

Early telegraph and phone lines were made of metal wire, but newer technologies are often "wireless". Instead of using wires or cables, radio or other signals are sent through the air.

Cables and Wires

Many telephone networks still have some copper wires in place, but these are slowly being replaced by new fibre-optic cables.

Optical fibres are strands of glass or plastic, as thin as a human hair, inside a protective coating. They are used in bundles of hundreds or thousands, bound into a cable.

Copper wires carry information as pulses (little bursts) of electrical charge. Fibre-optic cables carry information as light pulses.

Optical fibres, made of glass, carry information coded as pulses of light.

 Looking Forward

Glass Fibre with No Glass

In an optical fibre, the light travels down the strand of glass by bouncing off the inside of the coating again and again. Although the glass is very pure, it does slow the light down a little.

Scientists have developed a new cable that doesn't have glass in the middle – instead, the light is sent through a vacuum, or empty space. There is nothing to slow down the light, and it travels at 300,000 kilometres per second.

Looking Back

Early Cables

The very first wires laid under the sea to carry telegraphs quickly failed because they weren't properly protected against water. The first cable between England and France failed after eight days, and the first transatlantic cable lasted for only three weeks.

Once cables were laid inside a latex sheath, they worked properly. Later insulators, made of plastic, were even better. The first transatlantic fibre-optic cables were laid in 1988.

Tall towers are used to send out and boost radio signals.

Airwaves

Wireless communications are sent by radio waves, which travel through the air at the speed of light (see pages 10–11). Radio waves are part of the electromagnetic spectrum, which also includes visible and invisible light, and the microwaves we use for cooking.

A radio signal doesn't need to be sent along a particular pathway, like a cable. It is sent out into the air, or even into space, and picked up by any receiver that is tuned to accept it. Radio, television, mobile phones, some remote control boxes and wireless computer networks all use radio waves.

When you use a phone, the sound of your voice is converted into electrical signals. These travel at the speed of light along the telephone network. If phone calls travelled at the speed of sound, there would be a long gap between one person saying something and the other hearing it.

There's Nobody There ...

Many businesses no longer have lots of people answering by phone – they use computers instead. You might "talk" to a computer if you book cinema tickets over the phone or call a phone-in competition line. Instead of speaking to someone, you will be asked to make choices by pressing numbers on your phone.

Looking Forward

Voice recognition

Scientists are working on computer systems that can understand speech and could answer voice phone calls. Called "voice recognition", this is very difficult to get right. The computer needs to be able to tell the difference between words that sound similar, and to ignore extra noises, like "um" and "er". It must also deal with different accents and people who speak quickly or slowly.

A cordless phone can be carried around the home and used anywhere that is comfortable or convenient.

Right: People who work in call centres deal with phone enquiries or orders all day. Because phones offer instant communication around the world, many call centres are being moved to places such as India, where wages and rents are lower.

Not Just Voice

The phone network isn't used only for voice calls. It's also used to send fax messages.

Fax machines send an image of a piece of paper from one place to another. The sendor's fax machine scans the paper – it makes a picture of it, coded as a set of electrical pulses. The receiver's fax machine changes these electrical pulses back to an image and prints it out on paper.

Looking Back

Telex

Before fax was invented, there were two ways of getting a written message from one place to another using the phone lines – telegraph or telex. Telegraphs had to go through a main telegraph office to be converted from dots and dashes back to words, but telex could be sent directly.

Telex stands for *tele*printer *ex*change. The message is typed into a telex machine, which is like a mechanical typewriter. It is automatically typed out on another telex machine at the other end.

Radio

Radio can be transmitted through the air or through space. It can even pass through buildings and other solid objects. Most wireless communications use radio, although a few use infrared.

Radio Waves

Radio is transmitted as "waves" of energy. Radio waves can carry sound, pictures or computer data. They are sent out by a radio transmitter.

A radio signal is decoded by a radio receiver – it might be a mobile phone, a TV, a radio, or part of a computer network. The receiver changes the variations in the radio wave back into sound or data.

Digital Radio

Most radio transmitters can only send a radio signal fifty to sixty kilometres on land before it breaks up. National radio stations use extra transmitters around the country to boost the signal.

New satellite radio transmitters broadcast digital radio (see pages 16–17). The signal arrives from 35,000 kilometres above the Earth and is much clearer.

The voice of the DJ in this radio studio is broadcast as waves sent out by a radio transmitter. These are picked up by radio receivers in people's homes and cars.

You can also listen to radio stations on your computer to get a clear signal. You need to use the web page of the radio station and play it using your computer's sound system. The sound is carried as data over the Internet, just like pictures and text.

Technology in Action

Marconi and the First Radio

The possibility of radio was predicted in 1860, but it took until the 1890s to become real. Two men worked separately on radio, and both claimed to have invented it. They were Italian inventor Guglielmo Marconi and the Croatian Nikola Tesla, working in the USA.

Marconi sent the first signal across the English Channel in 1899, and the first signal across the Atlantic two years later. The message was the Morse code for the letter "S".

Guglielmo Marconi, photographed with his radio equipment. In 1909 he won a Nobel prize for Physics for his work on radio.

Radio School

The Alice Springs School of the Air has 140 pupils, but they live in an area of a million square kilometres in the Australian outback. They are too far away from each other to attend a school building.

Instead they use the Internet and two-way radio to share lessons with other children and teachers. The school broadcasts a message to all pupils each morning. Children have three class lessons a week and one individual lesson of ten minutes.

Mobile telephones help us to keep in touch wherever we are. Because they communicate with the phone network by radio, they don't need any wires or cables.

A man herding horses in the Andes, Chile, uses a mobile phone to communicate with other herders.

Cells and Bases

Mobile phones are sometimes called "cell phones" because the phone networks break each country into "cells", or small areas. Each cell has a base station that deals with all the calls and messages for each phone in its area. From the base station a call is passed onto the rest of the phone network or sent out to the phone that needs it.

To make or receive calls, a phone has to be near enough to a base station. This works well in most places, but in remote areas mobile phones sometimes don't work. And inside large buildings or under the ground there is often too much solid material for the radio waves to get through properly.

>>> Looking Forward

Dial-a-drink

We will soon be able to pay by mobile phone for parking, snacks and other cheap items. Swedish telephone company Nokia has developed a system that lets you press number buttons on the phone to order a drink from a vending machine. The cost of the item is charged to the phone bill.

Young people often like to play games on their mobile phones.

In some places, such as hospitals and aeroplanes, mobile phones aren't allowed because the radio signals might interfere with other equipment.

Fun and Games

The latest mobile phones have extra functions, such as games, built-in cameras, or radios. Some have multi-player games to play with other phone users.

The most advanced phones, called third-generation (3G) phones, can even receive short video clips. In Britain, the television channel ITV sends news bulletins that can be watched on 3G phones.

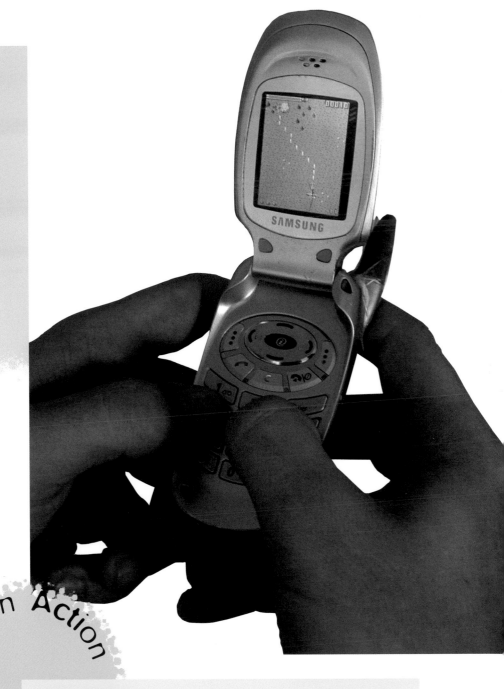

Technology in Action

Phone Music

Many people like to buy or compose new ring tones for their phones. In 2004, the German pop group Panda Babies became the first band to release an album only as polyphonic ring tones, with no CD available.

Polyphonic ring tones have high-quality sound, nearly as good as a CD. The Panda Babies album is downloaded from the Internet and can be played only on a phone.

Many people enjoy playing multi-player games on their phones, or sending text messages to each other.

When mobile phones were first developed, the phone companies added a way of sending text messages to help phone engineers set up and test networks. But text messaging became so popular with customers that it's now the most common use of mobile phones in some countries.

TXT 4 U

On early phones, you had to press a number key several times to get a single letter. Because it took a long time to key in a message, and messages could only be 163 characters long, people used abbreviations and developed a special "txt msg" shorthand language.

New phones use a system called "predictive text input". With this, you need to press a number key only once for each letter and the phone guesses which word you want. Many phones now allow longer messages too, automatically breaking them into a series of linked short messages.

Flight Information
Arriving at the airport to find your plane's delayed could soon be a thing of the past. On 1 August 2003, the two airports in Rome, Ciampino and Fiumicino, introduced a text message update service for people meeting or taking flights. For a small fee, up to four messages are sent giving up-to-date flight information.

PIX 4 U

Many phones have digital cameras, so that you can take a picture to send as a message or move to a computer. It's also possible to send pictures downloaded from a website.

The website of the National Gallery in London sells images of pictures in its collections which can be sent directly to your mobile phone.

This man is taking a photo with his phone of the religious festival Rathayatra.

Looking Back

Pager Language

Before text messaging, American teenagers used pagers to keep in touch with each other. Pagers are small electronic devices that can receive a short message in text or often just in numbers.

The codes teenagers used were based on the way some letters look like numbers. For example:
90*401773 means GO HOME

This is because "9" looks like "g"; "0" = "O"; "4" looks like "h" upside down; "177" looks very slightly like "m"; and "3" looks like "E" backwards.

Satellites

A satellite is something that goes around Earth or another planet. The moon is Earth's only natural satellite. Modern communications use artificial satellites to broadcast signals around the Earth.

Each of these Inmarsat-3 satellites covers part of the Earth's surface with its transmissions. Between them, they have the whole planet covered.

Our Presence in Space

Satellites are launched into space on the back of a rocket or in the space shuttle. There are currently around 26,000 satellites in orbit, including working satellites, old satellites no longer in use, and various bits of "space junk".

How We Use Satellites

Satellites have lots of uses. We use them to transmit phone, radio or TV signals. Others are used for navigation and locating positions on Earth. Some pick up distress signals broadcast in emergencies, letting rescuers know where help is needed so they can get there quickly.

Looking Back

Sputnik

The first artificial satellite was *Sputnik 1*, launched from the Soviet Union in 1957. It worked for only three weeks before its battery ran out. During this time it sent radio signals to Earth. These signals reported temperature changes measured by instruments on *Sputnik 1*. The tone of a "beep" varied to show the change in temperature. *Sputnik 1* burned up in the Earth's atmosphere after 92 days.

Satellites are also used for spying, military operations, watching climate change, and looking into space.

Where are You?

Global positioning systems (GPS) help us locate people or vehicles carrying special GPS devices. The position of a GPS device can be pinpointed exactly, using information collected from satellites.

Some mobile phones contain GPS devices. GPS is also used by courier services and the police for tracking vehicles, and by explorers, soldiers and others who go into dangerous areas from which they might need to be rescued.

Technology in Action

Where in the World?
In January 2004, fourteen fishermen were stranded on a lump of ice that broke free in Lake Erie, Ohio. They called for help using mobile phones, but could not say where they were. Luckily, the fishermen had GPS receivers and so coastguards could get straight to them using satellite information.

This field geologist can check his location using a hand-held GPS receiver. He is able to pinpoint where he is to within a hundred metres.

We all use television without a second thought – for news, education, entertainment, and even to receive information we don't really want, like advertisements.

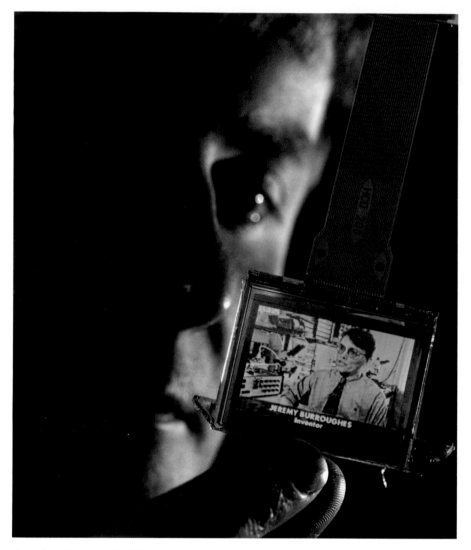

An ultra-thin plastic **TV** screen, only 2mm thick – the portable **TV** of the future?

Looking Forward

Converging Technologies
In the future, we are likely to use fewer electronic devices, but each one will have more functions. Already we can watch TV on our computers, or surf the web from a TV set.

In a few years, phones will be able to show good-quality video and we will be able to watch television on them, as well as use them for email and the web. There are mini-TVs that can be worn like a wristwatch, too.

How it Works

Television signals, like radio signals, were originally sent through the air and picked up by an aerial at each home that had a television. External television aerials are gradually disappearing as more and more people watch cable or satellite television.

Cable TV is transmitted through fibre-optic cables underground. To stop people watching the channels for free, they are sent in code – you need a set-top box to decode the channels to watch them.

Satellite TV is broadcast over a wide area by communications satellites. If you have a satellite dish to receive TV channels, you have to turn it so that it's facing the satellite that broadcasts the channels you want.

Technology in Action

British journalists working in the desert in Kuwait use technology linked by satellite to send video reports to London.

Digital TV

Digital TV uses a different method of sending the TV signal. It sends it in the form of separate tiny pulses rather than in continuous radio waves, which are "analogue signals". It produces a much sharper image than old-style, analogue TV.

Eventually, broadcasters will stop sending out analogue signals and everyone will need to have a digital TV to pick up TV programmes.

Embedded Journalists

The war in Iraq in 2003 saw journalists for TV and radio stations and newspapers working alongside ("embedded with") allied troops to report on the war.

Instead of sending their reports from a safe distance behind the action, they were on the front line, and had to use advanced communications technology to make and send their reports. Reports were transmitted directly from the front line by satellite and often broadcast live around the world.

The Internet

The Internet is the worldwide network of computers that is used for sharing and communicating information. Most people use the Internet for email and the World Wide Web.

Changing the World

Anyone can publish web pages. It means we can share our interests and problems with people around the world, and find information on any topic in a matter of seconds.

But the web means much more to people in some countries. It has changed the way we find out news and has made it much harder to keep secrets. Although some countries try to restrict Internet access, it's difficult to block it completely.

Web logs, or "blogs", are a kind of online diary. Web logs kept by US soldiers in Iraq in 2003 gave an account of everyday life in a war while it was happening in a way that was not possible before.

In a **cybercafe**, a customer can use the Internet to browse the web or send email.

Moving Life Online

More and more of our daily lives can be carried out over the Internet. We can now shop, manage our money, book tickets for travel and events, play games and communicate instantly with distant friends. We can even diagnose our illnesses without visiting a doctor.

Already we can add our names to international petitions, and soon we may be able to vote in elections online.

With a credit card, it's easy to shop online, ordering tickets or goods from a web page.

Looking Back

Predicting the World Wide Web

The World Wide Web started in 1990, but in 1945 an American, Vannevar Bush, suggested a computer system that would show people linked pages of information and pictures. His idea was far ahead of its time, although his system looked nothing like the computers we use for web browsing now.

Looking Forward

The Interplanetary Internet

Soon the World Wide Web may not be restricted to this world. There are plans to put computers on other planets in the solar system. To start with they would communicate by radio, but eventually they would use laser light.

First, we're likely to see a set of relay satellites around Mars that could be used for spacecraft to communicate with Earth. Work may start in 2005, but a full interplanetary network won't be in place before 2040.

21

Talking Online

"Chat" used to mean just speaking. Now we can "chat" online by typing a conversation. This can be a private chat between friends who have agreed to talk to each other, or a discussion in a public chat room where anyone can join in.

Each person types messages from their own computer, and they are shown on the computers of everyone else taking part in the chat.

Who are You Talking To?

We can use online chat to talk to people we already know, or use a chat room to "meet" people who share a particular interest. Online celebrity chats give people the chance to put questions to famous writers, singers, actors or politicians.

Chat can be for fun, or can be a way of passing on or gathering serious information. For example, Internet support groups for people with rare medical problems bring together sufferers from around the world so that they can share experiences and solutions to problems.

Looking Back

Bulletin Boards

Before online chat and web logs, one way in which people shared news and information on the Internet was by using bulletin boards. These are a bit like electronic noticeboards. Anyone can "post" a message, and everyone else can read it.

In 1991, during the final months of the Communist regime in the Soviet Union, many Russians posted information on bulletin boards or sent emails to friends in other countries, giving them valuable information about what was happening.

Chatting online is a good way of keeping in touch with distant friends and relatives. It's cheaper than a long-distance phone call and quicker than a letter.

Safe Chatting

On the Internet, people can easily pretend to be someone they're not. It's very important that young people use moderated chat rooms – services that are monitored to make sure nothing offensive or dangerous is said. It's safest to chat only to people you already know well.

This Cybiko wireless computer for children can be used for email, chat, games and the World Wide Web.

>> Looking Forward

Smile!

New developments could make chat more of a face-to-face experience. One plan is to take a digital photo of a person's face and reduce it to the most important parts: the eyes, lips, nose and eyebrows.

Such a small image could be transmitted over the Internet quickly enough to work as a real-time, moving smilie, showing emotions during an online chat.

23

We can use telecoms technologies to help us see what's going on in places we can't get to. For many of us, that might mean looking at a web page to see a picture sent from a special place or event.

This man, in a cybercafe in Moscow, Russia, is watching a live webcast of an interview with the Russian president, Vladimir Putin.

Webcams and Webcasts

A webcam is a digital camera linked to a web page so that it shows an up-to-date picture of somewhere. For example, when the panda in San Diego Zoo had a baby in August 2003, the zoo set up a webcam so that people around the world could watch the baby grow. The panda cam was so popular, other zoos followed the example.

A webcast is a broadcast, like a TV programme, that is put out on the World Wide Web. To watch the webcast, you just need to open the right web page. Webcasts of sporting events, carnivals and rock concerts mean people who can't get to the venue can still enjoy the event.

Keeping an Eye on Things

Pictures sent from remote cameras can be used for spying and surveillance. The pictures can be sent over the Internet, like a webcast or webcam, or they can be sent by radio to a receiver.

Looking Forward

Roboroach and Roborat

Scientists are using implants to make remote-controlled cockroaches and rats that can be steered into buildings or disaster sites.

The cockroaches, the work of a team in Japan, will carry minute cameras and microphones in a "backpack". They can be used for spying or to help locate people trapped in rubble after an earthquake or explosion.

The rats, created in New York, are controlled by electronic impulses to their brains. When they obey the impulse, they are rewarded with a pleasant feeling.

Experts in California, USA, test the Pyramid Rover. The robot was sent to explore an air shaft in the Queen's Chamber of Egypt's Great Pyramid.

Technology in Action

Exploring the Mystery of the Great Pyramid

On 18 September 2002, archaeologists sent a remote-controlled robot into a mysterious tunnel in an Egyptian pyramid. The tunnel ended in a sealed door.

Following radioed instructions, the robot drilled a hole in the door and poked through a fibre-optic camera to look into the room for the first time in 4,500 years. They found only another door, so they will have to do further work to discover the pyramid's secrets.

In the future, we won't need to be at home to control what happens in our houses. It will be possible to turn equipment on and off remotely.

This kitchen table with a touch-screen surface is part of a display of how our homes may look after 2010. People can access the Internet by touching the table.

Phone Home

Some appliances in our homes will soon be controlled by mobile phone. You will be able to turn up the heating before getting home if the weather gets colder, set the DVD recorder, or turn on the oven ready to heat up a take-away you've just picked up.

And if someone comes to the door while you're out, you'll be able to see and talk to them from a web page linked to the security system. Some new houses in Australia are already being built with these capabilities.

Talking Fridges

Scientists are working on domestic appliances that can "talk" to each other without people around. They are developing fridges that can check what food is left in them, and order more over the Internet. To let the fridge "know" what it contains, you will need to scan the barcode on the food you put in and take out.

Home Help
People with disabilities are being helped at home by remote-controlled and wireless equipment. In a specially equipped home, radio and infrared remote control units can be used to open and close windows or curtains, operate doors and locks, adjust the heating, and control music or TV channels in all rooms.

Houses can also have special alarm systems to detect if the person living there has had an accident, and can call help if needed.

We all use remote controls for the TV, and sometimes for playstations and stereos. Soon, we'll be using them to control other equipment in our homes.

Looking Back

Remote Control TVs
Remote control was used by the German military to control speed boats in the First World War. It was first used in homes to open garage doors in the 1940s.

The first wireless TV remote control, developed in 1955, was operated by a flashlight. The light was detected by sensors on the screen. Unfortunately, bright sunlight on the screen could switch channels.

The first TV remote to use ultrasound (very high-pitched sound that we can't hear) was designed in 1956. In the 1980s, infrared took over from ultrasound.

Communicating with Other Worlds

The Parkes radio telescope in New South Wales, Australia. Its dish is sixty-four metres across, and it is used to pick up radio waves from space.

As we explore further and further into space, we will need to invent new ways of communicating to keep in touch with spacecraft millions of kilometres away.

Radio from Space

Radio telescopes pick up radio signals from deep space. We use these to find out about the history of the universe and the make-up of distant stars. We also send our own signals into space in the hope of getting a reply from intelligent beings elsewhere in the universe.

 Looking Forward

Sending Secrets through Space

Even though we can't yet reach distant stars, scientists are thinking of how to keep messages safe when they send them between galaxies. One suggestion is that a message could be split into two beams of photons (tiny particles of light) and bounced off mirrors in space, only coming back together at the destination.

28

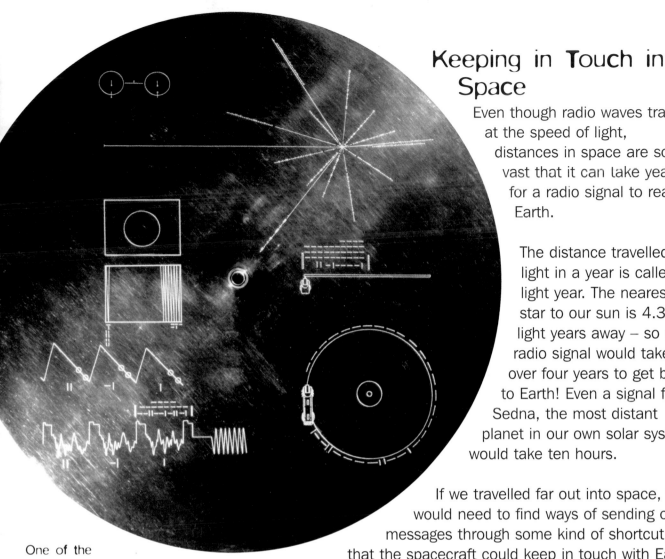

Keeping in Touch in Space

Even though radio waves travel at the speed of light, distances in space are so vast that it can take years for a radio signal to reach Earth.

The distance travelled by light in a year is called a light year. The nearest star to our sun is 4.3 light years away – so a radio signal would take over four years to get back to Earth! Even a signal from Sedna, the most distant planet in our own solar system, would take ten hours.

If we travelled far out into space, we would need to find ways of sending our messages through some kind of shortcut, so that the spacecraft could keep in touch with Earth.

One of the Golden Records – the gold discs carried by the *Voyager 1* spacecraft that has been sent out into space with messages for any beings that find it.

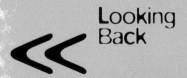

Looking Back

Hello, Universe

The spacecraft *Voyager 1* was sent to explore distant space twenty-six years ago. Signals to control it now take more than twelve hours to reach the craft and are very weak when they arrive.

Voyager 1 is reaching the edge of our solar system. It carries messages for any alien spacecraft it may meet. These are sounds, words and pictures stored on gold discs. They include greetings in fifty-four languages and a map of where Earth is in the universe.

Timeline

1200 BCE The ancient Greeks use fires to send signals over long distances.

37 BCE The Romans use a "heliograph", a system of mirrors to send messages with flashes of sunlight.

1793 The first commercial semaphore system is set up in France. Two movable mechanical arms on a pole are used to signal letters of the alphabet, according to their positions.

1830 Joseph Henry rings a bell one mile away by sending an electrical signal along a wire.

1838 The first commercial telegraph line is built, between Washington and Baltimore, USA.

1876 Alexander Graham Bell patents the telephone.

1878 The first telephone exchange opens, in New Haven, Connecticut, USA.

1895 Radio is invented.

1920 The first public radio broadcasts, started by Marconi in Britain.

1936 The first public TV broadcasts begin in Britain by the BBC.

1953 Colour television is developed in the USA.

1957 The first artificial satellite, *Sputnik 1*, is launched by the Soviet Union.

1962 The first communications satellite goes into service.

1966 Optical fibres are developed.

1969 The formation of ARPANET, which linked the computers of four universities together and formed the basis of the Internet; email was first used on ARPANET in the same year.

1978 The first GPS system is developed by the US Air Force.

1979 The first mobile phone is developed in the USA.

1983 The Internet evolves from ARPANET; mobile phones become available to the public.

1990 The invention of the World Wide Web by British physicist Tim Berners-Lee.

1993 The first web browser is developed that can show text and pictures together.

1997 The development of WAP (wireless application protocol) means that mobile phones can be used to browse the web.

Glossary

aerial A wire or metal rod used to transmit or receive radio or television signals.

analogue Information in the form of a continuous stream or wave.

archaeologist A person who studies the past by finding and examining very old objects and buildings.

base station A base station provides a communications service for all the mobile phones in a cell, and forms their link to the larger phone network.

broadcast Send out a television or radio programme.

cell An area defined for the operation of mobile phones, that is served by a base station.

character A letter, number or punctuation mark.

data Information, or the raw facts and figures that can be turned into meaningful information.

digital Information in the form of separate tiny chunks or pulses.

digital photo A photograph that is recorded digitally on a computer rather than on a photographic film.

electromagnetic spectrum The range of energy that exists as waves, including visible and invisible light, X-rays, and radio waves.

fibre-optic cable Cable made of bunches of optical fibres – thin glass fibres used to carry data as pulses of light.

implant Something artificial that is put into the body.

infrared Energy in the form of light which is invisible to people, but can be felt as heat and (with special goggles) used to show things in the dark. Infrared can be used for remote control over a short distance, but it can't go round corners or through solid objects.

insulators Materials that can't carry electricity (or heat). Insulators are used around cables that carry electricity to keep the electricity in the cable.

latex A material made of rubber or artificial rubber.

network A set of computers, phones or other equipment, linked together to communicate and share information.

online Connected to the Internet.

pulse A small burst of activity or energy, often of electricity or light.

receiver A piece of equipment set up to accept signals (such as radio or television signals).

satellite A natural or artificial object that goes around a planet.

scan Make an image from something.

set-top box A box for decoding cable television signals.

Soviet Union Also known as the USSR (Union of Soviet Socialist Republics), a country formed from the territories of the Russian Empire in 1917, which lasted until 1991.

space junk Items we have left in space that are no longer used or needed.

stylus A small plastic stick that looks like a pen and is used to point to things on, or write on, a touch-sensitive screen.

surveillance Watching someone or something, usually secretly.

transatlantic Crossing the Atlantic ocean.

transmitter A piece of equipment used to send out radio waves so that they can be picked up at a distant location.

tuned Set to pick up and make sense of a particular source or type of radio wave.

typewriter A mechanical or electric machine for producing text that looks as though it is printed. It works by pressing a metal key with a single character against a ribbon treated with ink so that it presses onto a piece of paper and makes a mark in the shape of the character.

Further Information

Further Reading

How Things Work by John Farndon (Miles Kelly Science Library, 2004)

Internet Technologies (Tomorrow's Science) by Anne Rooney (Chrysalis, 2003)

Telecommunications (21st Century Science series) by Simon Maddison (Franklin Watts, 2003)

How Things Work: An Illustrated Encyclopedia of the Amazing World of Technology by Chris Oxlade (Lorenz Books, 2002)

1960s the Satellite Age (20th Century Media series) by Steve Parker (Heinemann Library, 2002)

The Usborne Internet-linked Science Encyclopedia by Judy Tatchell (Usborne Publishing, 2002)

Pictures Through the Air: The Story of John Logie Baird (Super Scientists series) by Anthony Masters (Hodder Wayland, 2001)

CD ROMs

Become a Science Explorer (Dorling Kindersley)

The New Way Things Work (Dorling Kindersley)

Websites

www.howstuffworks.com
Explains how many items of telecommunications equipment work.

http://voyager.jpl.nasa.gov/
Find out about how we communicate with spacecraft sent from Earth.

http://news.bbc.co.uk/1/hi/technology/1478157.stm
Keep up to date on telecoms stories with an archive of stories to listen to or read from the BBC's programme about digital technologies, *Go Digital*.

Index

Page numbers in **bold** refer to illustrations.